MY BODY Inside and Out!

My Amazing Sense of Sight

by Ruth Owen

Consultant:

Suzy Gazlay, MA
Recipient, Presidential Award for Excellence in Science Teaching

Published in 2014 by Ruby Tuesday Books Ltd.

Copyright © 2014 Ruby Tuesday Books Ltd.

All rights reserved. No part of this publication may be reproduced in whole or in part, stored in any retrieval system, or transmitted in any form or by any means, electronic, mechanical, photocopying, recording, or otherwise, without written permission from the publisher.

Editor: Mark J. Sachner
Designer: Emma Randall
Production: John Lingham

Photo credits:
Shutterstock: 1, 4–5, 6–7, 8–9, 10–11, 12–13, 14–15, 16–17, 18, 19 (bottom), 20–21, 23; Superstock: Cover, 19 (top).

Library of Congress Control Number: 2013919035

ISBN 978-1-909673-42-7

Printed and published in the United States of America

For further information including rights and permissions requests, please contact our Customer Service Department at 877-337-8577.

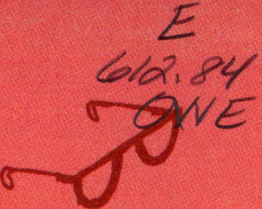

Contents

Seeing Your World 4
Light in Your World 6
Check Out Your Eyes 8
What's Inside Your Eyeball? 10
Making Pictures 12
Your Brain Gets Busy 14
Amazing Eyeballs 16
Help with Seeing 18
Take Care of Your Eyes 20

Glossary 22
Index 24
Read More 24
Learn More Online 24

Words shown in **bold** in the text are explained in the glossary.

Seeing Your World

From the moment you open your eyes in the morning, you see the world around you.

Your **sense** of sight helps you get dressed, play sports, read books, and see your friends.

It keeps you safe by letting you look for cars as you cross the street.

You can even see your own face when you look in a mirror.

Each day your eyes see thousands of colors, shapes, and movements.

Just how does this amazing sense work, though? Let's find out!

Your body has five senses. These are seeing, hearing, smelling, tasting, and touching. Your senses help keep you safe. They also help you enjoy the world around you.

Light in Your World

In order to see the world around us, we need light.

In the daytime, light usually comes from the Sun.

At night, we switch on lamps and other types of lighting.

When light from the Sun or a lamp hits an object, the light bounces or reflects off the object.

Your eyes capture this reflected light.

Then your eyes and brain work together to allow you to see the object.

If you stand in a completely dark room, you can't see the objects around you. That's because there is no light reflecting off the objects. Your eyes are still working, but there is no light for your eyes to capture.

Check Out Your Eyes

Without your eyes, or eyeballs, you wouldn't be able to see everything that's going on around you.

Your eyeballs are safely tucked inside your head, so you can only see a small part of them.

The white part of your eye that you can see is a tough, outer covering called the **sclera**.

The round, colored part of your eyeball is called the **iris**.

In the center of your iris is a **pupil**.

Your pupil looks black, but it's actually a small, round opening with an important job to do.

Each of your eyeballs is about the size of a ping-pong ball.

The irises of a person's eyes can be brown, blue, or green.

Sclera

Iris

Pupil

Every time you blink, your eyelids clean your eyes and **moisten** them. If you didn't blink, your eyes would get dirty and dry.

Eyelid

You can make yourself blink, but your eyelids also blink without you even thinking about it.

What's Inside Your Eyeball?

Each of your eyes is covered with a see-through, dome-shaped layer of **tissue** called the **cornea**.

The cornea captures light and directs it into your eye through your pupil.

Once the light is inside your eye, it hits another see-through part called the **lens**.

The job of your lens is to focus light onto the back of your eyeball.

This back part of your eye is called the **retina**.

Tiny muscles in your irises can make your pupils get bigger or smaller. If light is very bright, your pupils get smaller. This stops too much light from entering your eyes.

Small pupil   Big pupil

If there is not enough light, your pupils get bigger. This lets as much light into your eyes as possible.

Making Pictures

Each of your retinas contains millions of tiny **cells** called **rods** and **cones**.

The light that your eye has captured hits these cells.

The hardworking rods and cones collect lots of information from the light.

Then they use the information to create a picture.

The picture is sent as messages along your **optic nerve** to your brain.

The picture created by your retina is actually upside-down!

Look at this dog and ball. The reflected light from the picture is entering each of your eyes and hitting its retina.

It's the job of the cones in the retina to detect the colors in the reflected light. The rods detect black, white, and gray. They also detect the shapes of things.

Your rods and cones use the information they collect to send a picture of the dog and ball to your brain.

Each of your retinas contains about 120 million rods and 7 million cones!

Your Brain Gets Busy

The upside-down picture created by your retina speeds along your optic nerve.

When your brain receives the picture, it flips it the right way up.

Then, your brain figures out what the picture shows.

In an instant, you see the object you were looking at!

Your amazing eyes and brain help you see shapes, movements, and about 10 million different colors!

Brain

Every second your eyes are open, pictures of your world are zooming from your eyes to your brain.

Amazing Eyeballs

Look up. Look down. Look at something far away or something that's near to you.

Your busy eyes have lots of ways to make sure you see everything around you.

To do their job, the lenses in your eyes can actually change shape.

To make sure you can see objects that are very near to you, your lenses get thicker.

When you want to look at something that's far away, your lenses get thinner.

Each of your eyeballs has six tiny muscles attached to it. The muscles help you move your eyes up and down and side to side.

A model of an *eyeball*

Muscles

When you look at the dog that's near to you, this is what you see.

The lenses in your eyes get thicker.

When you look at the sunflowers that are far away, this is what you see.

The lenses in your eyes get thinner.

Help with Seeing

Not everyone sees in the same way.

Some people can't see things clearly that are far away.

Others can see things in the distance, but have trouble seeing things that are up close.

These differences in sight can happen if parts of a person's eyes are not doing their jobs.

Usually, it's possible for a person to wear glasses or **contact lenses** to improve how he or she sees.

The lenses in our eyes may not focus light onto our retinas properly. This means that pictures created by the retinas are fuzzy. Wearing glasses or contact lenses helps fix this.

Often people's eyes don't see as well as they get older. Think of all the adults you know. How many of them wear glasses?

Some people are blind and have a guide dog. A guide dog is trained to keep its owner safe. Guide dogs can help their owners cross the street and lead them onto buses and trains.

A guide dog

Take Care of Your Eyes

All day, every day, your eyes are keeping you safe and helping you have fun.

In fact, your sense of sight is the busiest of all your senses.

It's very important, therefore, that you take good care of your eyes.

If you play sports such as football or hockey, you can wear a helmet with a shield to protect your eyes.

On sunny days, wear sunglasses to protect your eyes from bright sunlight.

Take care of your amazing eyes, and they'll keep on taking care of you!

If you watch TV or look at a computer for too long, it will make your eyes tired. Every 20 to 30 minutes, try to give your eyes a rest and spend some time away from the screen.

If your eyes hurt or feel tired, tell a grown-up. Also, tell your teacher if you're having trouble seeing the board at school, or seeing the words in your books. Then you can arrange to see an eye doctor and get an eye check-up.

Glossary

cells (SELZ)
Very tiny parts of a living thing. Your bones, muscles, skin, hair, and every part of you are made of cells.

cones (KOHNZ)
Cells in your retinas that detect colors in the light that enters your eyes.

contact lenses (KON-takt LEN-ziz)
Small, see-through discs that some people wear on their eyes to help improve their sight. Contact lenses are placed onto a person's corneas.

cornea (KOR-nee-uh)
A see-through, dome-shaped layer of tissue that covers your iris and pupil. The cornea captures light and directs it into your eye.

iris (EYE-riss)
The colored, circular part of your eye.

lens (LENZ)
A see-through part of your eye that focuses light onto the retina.

moisten (MOI-suhn)
Make something slightly wet.

optic nerve (OP-tik NURV)
A group of cells that carry information from the retina in your eye to your brain.

pupil (PYOO-puhl)
A small, round opening in the center of your eye. The pupil looks black, but it's actually a small hole that allows light to enter your eye.

retina (RET-in-uh)
The back wall of your eyeball. Cells, called rods and cones, in your retinas take the light that enters your eyes and help turn it into the things you see.

rods (RODZ)
Cells in your retinas that detect shapes in the light that enters your eyes. Rods also detect black, white, and gray.

sclera (SKLER-uh)
The white part of your eye. The sclera is a tough outer covering for the eyeball.

sense (SENSS)
One of the five ways that you collect information about the world around you. Your senses are seeing, hearing, smelling, tasting, and touching.

tissue (TISH-yoo)
A group of connected cells in your body that work together. Cells are very tiny parts of a living thing. Skin tissue, for example, is made up of skin cells.

Index

B
blindness 19
blinking 9
brain 6, 12–13, 14–15

C
caring for eyes 20–21
cells 12
colors 4, 13, 14
cones 12–13
contact lenses 18
corneas 10–11

D
doctors 21

E
eyelids 9
eyes 4, 6–7, 8–9, 10–11, 12–13, 14–15, 16–17, 18–19, 20–21

G
glasses 18–19
guide dogs 19

I
irises 8–9, 10–11

L
lenses 10–11, 12, 16–17, 18
light 6–7, 10–11, 12–13, 18

M
movements 4, 14
muscles 16

O
optic nerves 12, 14

P
pupils 8–9, 10–11

R
reflected light 6–7, 13
retinas 10–11, 12–13, 14, 18
rods 12–13

S
sclera 8–9, 11
senses 4–5, 20
shapes 4, 13, 14
Sun, the 6–7, 20
sunglasses 20

Read More

Lawrence, Ellen. *Light (Fundamental Experiments)*. New York: Bearport Publishing (2014).

Rissman, Rebecca. *Seeing (The Five Senses)*. North Mankato, MN: Heinemann-Raintree (2010).

Learn More Online

To learn more about your sense of sight, go to
www.rubytuesdaybooks.com/mybodysight

1-14-15